This Cigar Aficionado Log

Belongs To:

_____

EAT.
SLEEP.
CIGAR.
REPEAT.

"I started smoking these little Italian cigars just so there was some of that smell in the air."

Francis Ford Coppola

TASTE NOTES

I'M FULL BODIED
& A LITTLE
LEATHERY...

LIKE A FINE
Cigar

CIGAR NAME: _____

MAKER: _____   **PRICE:** _____

ORIGIN: _____   **DATE:** _____

LENGTH: _____   **RING SIZE:** _____

SHAPE: _____   **BUY AGAIN?** _____

AFFIX CIGAR LABEL HERE

RATING
☆☆☆☆☆

FULL

MED/FULL

MEDIUM

MILD

LIGHT

FLAVOR CHART 0=LEAST 5=MOST					
BITTER					
CHOCOLATE					
EARTHY					
FRUITY					
HERBAL					
LEATHER					
NUTTY					
SPICY					
SWEET					
TOFFEE					
TROPICAL					
VANILLA					
WOODY					

TASTE NOTES

_____
_____
_____
_____
_____
_____
_____
_____
_____
_____
_____
_____
_____
_____
_____
_____

Cigar aficionado

CIGAR NAME: _____

MAKER: _____ **PRICE:** _____

ORIGIN: _____ **DATE:** _____

LENGTH: _____ **RING SIZE:** _____

SHAPE: _____ **BUY AGAIN?** _____

AFFIX CIGAR LABEL HERE

RATING
☆☆☆☆☆

FULL

MED/FULL

MEDIUM

MILD

LIGHT

FLAVOR CHART 0=LEAST 5=MOST						
BITTER						
CHOCOLATE						
EARTHY						
FRUITY						
HERBAL						
LEATHER						
NUTTY						
SPICY						
SWEET						
TOFFEE						
TROPICAL						
VANILLA						
WOODY						

TASTE NOTES

They see me rollin'

CIGAR NAME: _____

MAKER: _____   **PRICE:** _____

ORIGIN: _____   **DATE:** _____

LENGTH: _____   **RING SIZE:** _____

SHAPE: _____   **BUY AGAIN?** _____

AFFIX CIGAR LABEL HERE

RATING
☆☆☆☆☆

FULL

MED/FULL

MEDIUM

MILD

LIGHT

FLAVOR CHART 0=LEAST 5=MOST					
BITTER					
CHOCOLATE					
EARTHY					
FRUITY					
HERBAL					
LEATHER					
NUTTY					
SPICY					
SWEET					
TOFFEE					
TROPICAL					
VANILLA					
WOODY					

TASTE NOTES

A **Cigar** IN HAND IS BETTER THAN TWO IN THE HUMIDOR

CIGAR NAME:

MAKER: _____   **PRICE:** _____

ORIGIN: _____   **DATE:** _____

LENGTH: _____   **RING SIZE:** _____

SHAPE: _____   **BUY AGAIN?** _____

AFFIX CIGAR LABEL HERE

RATING
☆☆☆☆☆

FULL

MED/FULL

MEDIUM

MILD

LIGHT

FLAVOR CHART 0=LEAST 5=MOST					
BITTER					
CHOCOLATE					
EARTHY					
FRUITY					
HERBAL					
LEATHER					
NUTTY					
SPICY					
SWEET					
TOFFEE					
TROPICAL					
VANILLA					
WOODY					

TASTE NOTES

CIGAR NAME: _____

MAKER: _____ **PRICE:** _____

ORIGIN: _____ **DATE:** _____

LENGTH: _____ **RING SIZE:** _____

SHAPE: _____ **BUY AGAIN?** _____

AFFIX CIGAR LABEL HERE

RATING
☆☆☆☆☆

FULL

MED/FULL

MEDIUM

MILD

LIGHT

FLAVOR CHART 0=LEAST 5=MOST					
BITTER					
CHOCOLATE					
EARTHY					
FRUITY					
HERBAL					
LEATHER					
NUTTY					
SPICY					
SWEET					
TOFFEE					
TROPICAL					
VANILLA					
WOODY					

TASTE NOTES

me time

CIGAR NAME: _____

MAKER: _____   **PRICE:** _____

ORIGIN: _____   **DATE:** _____

LENGTH: _____   **RING SIZE:** _____

SHAPE: _____   **BUY AGAIN?** _____

AFFIX CIGAR LABEL HERE

RATING
☆☆☆☆☆

FULL	
MED/FULL	
MEDIUM	
MILD	
LIGHT	

FLAVOR CHART 0=LEAST 5=MOST					
BITTER					
CHOCOLATE					
EARTHY					
FRUITY					
HERBAL					
LEATHER					
NUTTY					
SPICY					
SWEET					
TOFFEE					
TROPICAL					
VANILLA					
WOODY					

TASTE NOTES

_____
_____
_____
_____
_____
_____
_____
_____
_____
_____
_____
_____
_____
_____
_____
_____

REAL MEN SMOKE
CIGARS

CIGAR NAME: _____

MAKER: _____ **PRICE:** _____

ORIGIN: _____ **DATE:** _____

LENGTH: _____ **RING SIZE:** _____

SHAPE: _____ **BUY AGAIN?** _____

AFFIX CIGAR LABEL HERE

RATING
☆☆☆☆☆

FULL

MED/FULL

MEDIUM

MILD

LIGHT

FLAVOR CHART 0=LEAST 5=MOST					
BITTER					
CHOCOLATE					
EARTHY					
FRUITY					
HERBAL					
LEATHER					
NUTTY					
SPICY					
SWEET					
TOFFEE					
TROPICAL					
VANILLA					
WOODY					

TASTE NOTES

_____

_____

_____

_____

_____

_____

_____

_____

_____

_____

_____

_____

_____

_____

_____

_____

CIGAR NAME: _____

MAKER: _____ **PRICE:** _____

ORIGIN: _____ **DATE:** _____

LENGTH: _____ **RING SIZE:** _____

SHAPE: _____ **BUY AGAIN?** _____

AFFIX CIGAR LABEL HERE

RATING
☆☆☆☆☆

FULL

MED/FULL

MEDIUM

MILD

LIGHT

FLAVOR CHART 0=LEAST 5=MOST					
BITTER					
CHOCOLATE					
EARTHY					
FRUITY					
HERBAL					
LEATHER					
NUTTY					
SPICY					
SWEET					
TOFFEE					
TROPICAL					
VANILLA					
WOODY					

TASTE NOTES

I'M FULL BODIED & A LITTLE LEATHERY... LIKE A FINE Cigar

CIGAR NAME: _____

MAKER: _____ **PRICE:** _____

ORIGIN: _____ **DATE:** _____

LENGTH: _____ **RING SIZE:** _____

SHAPE: _____ **BUY AGAIN?** _____

AFFIX CIGAR LABEL HERE

RATING
☆☆☆☆☆

FULL

MED/FULL

MEDIUM

MILD

LIGHT

FLAVOR CHART 0=LEAST 5=MOST					
BITTER					
CHOCOLATE					
EARTHY					
FRUITY					
HERBAL					
LEATHER					
NUTTY					
SPICY					
SWEET					
TOFFEE					
TROPICAL					
VANILLA					
WOODY					

TASTE NOTES

CIGAR NAME: _____

MAKER: _____ **PRICE:** _____

ORIGIN: _____ **DATE:** _____

LENGTH: _____ **RING SIZE:** _____

SHAPE: _____ **BUY AGAIN?** _____

AFFIX CIGAR LABEL HERE

RATING
☆☆☆☆☆

FULL

MED/FULL

MEDIUM

MILD

LIGHT

FLAVOR CHART 0=LEAST 5=MOST						
BITTER						
CHOCOLATE						
EARTHY						
FRUITY						
HERBAL						
LEATHER						
NUTTY						
SPICY						
SWEET						
TOFFEE						
TROPICAL						
VANILLA						
WOODY						

TASTE NOTES

CIGAR NAME: _____

MAKER: _____   **PRICE:** _____

ORIGIN: _____   **DATE:** _____

LENGTH: _____   **RING SIZE:** _____

SHAPE: _____   **BUY AGAIN?** _____

AFFIX CIGAR LABEL HERE

RATING
☆☆☆☆☆

FULL

MED/FULL

MEDIUM

MILD

LIGHT

FLAVOR CHART 0=LEAST 5=MOST						
BITTER						
CHOCOLATE						
EARTHY						
FRUITY						
HERBAL						
LEATHER						
NUTTY						
SPICY						
SWEET						
TOFFEE						
TROPICAL						
VANILLA						
WOODY						

TASTE NOTES

A
Cigar
IN
HAND
IS BETTER THAN TWO
IN THE HUMIDOR

CIGAR NAME: _____

MAKER: _____ **PRICE:** _____

ORIGIN: _____ **DATE:** _____

LENGTH: _____ **RING SIZE:** _____

SHAPE: _____ **BUY AGAIN?** _____

AFFIX CIGAR LABEL HERE

RATING
☆☆☆☆☆

FULL

MED/FULL

MEDIUM

MILD

LIGHT

FLAVOR CHART 0=LEAST 5=MOST						
BITTER						
CHOCOLATE						
EARTHY						
FRUITY						
HERBAL						
LEATHER						
NUTTY						
SPICY						
SWEET						
TOFFEE						
TROPICAL						
VANILLA						
WOODY						

TASTE NOTES

_____

_____

_____

_____

_____

_____

_____

_____

_____

_____

_____

_____

_____

_____

CIGAR NAME: _____

MAKER: _____ **PRICE:** _____

ORIGIN: _____ **DATE:** _____

LENGTH: _____ **RING SIZE:** _____

SHAPE: _____ **BUY AGAIN?** _____

AFFIX CIGAR LABEL HERE

RATING
☆☆☆☆☆

FULL

MED/FULL

MEDIUM

MILD

LIGHT

FLAVOR CHART 0=LEAST 5=MOST						
BITTER						
CHOCOLATE						
EARTHY						
FRUITY						
HERBAL						
LEATHER						
NUTTY						
SPICY						
SWEET						
TOFFEE						
TROPICAL						
VANILLA						
WOODY						

TASTE NOTES

me time

CIGAR NAME: _____

MAKER: _____ **PRICE:** _____

ORIGIN: _____ **DATE:** _____

LENGTH: _____ **RING SIZE:** _____

SHAPE: _____ **BUY AGAIN?** _____

AFFIX CIGAR LABEL HERE

RATING
☆☆☆☆☆

FULL

MED/FULL

MEDIUM

MILD

LIGHT

FLAVOR CHART 0=LEAST 5=MOST						
BITTER						
CHOCOLATE						
EARTHY						
FRUITY						
HERBAL						
LEATHER						
NUTTY						
SPICY						
SWEET						
TOFFEE						
TROPICAL						
VANILLA						
WOODY						

TASTE NOTES

REAL MEN SMOKE

CIGARS

CIGAR NAME: _____

MAKER: _____ **PRICE:** _____

ORIGIN: _____ **DATE:** _____

LENGTH: _____ **RING SIZE:** _____

SHAPE: _____ **BUY AGAIN?** _____

AFFIX CIGAR LABEL HERE

RATING
☆☆☆☆☆

FULL

MED/FULL

MEDIUM

MILD

LIGHT

FLAVOR CHART 0=LEAST 5=MOST					
BITTER					
CHOCOLATE					
EARTHY					
FRUITY					
HERBAL					
LEATHER					
NUTTY					
SPICY					
SWEET					
TOFFEE					
TROPICAL					
VANILLA					
WOODY					

TASTE NOTES

_____
_____
_____
_____
_____
_____
_____
_____
_____
_____
_____
_____
_____
_____

CIGAR NAME: _____

MAKER: _____   PRICE: _____

ORIGIN: _____   DATE: _____

LENGTH: _____   RING SIZE: _____

SHAPE: _____   BUY AGAIN? _____

AFFIX CIGAR LABEL HERE

RATING
☆☆☆☆☆

	FULL
	MED/FULL
	MEDIUM
	MILD
	LIGHT

FLAVOR CHART 0=LEAST 5=MOST						
BITTER						
CHOCOLATE						
EARTHY						
FRUITY						
HERBAL						
LEATHER						
NUTTY						
SPICY						
SWEET						
TOFFEE						
TROPICAL						
VANILLA						
WOODY						

TASTE NOTES

I'M FULL BODIED & A LITTLE LEATHERY... LIKE A FINE *Cigar*

CIGAR NAME: _____

MAKER: _____ **PRICE:** _____

ORIGIN: _____ **DATE:** _____

LENGTH: _____ **RING SIZE:** _____

SHAPE: _____ **BUY AGAIN?** _____

AFFIX CIGAR LABEL HERE

RATING
☆☆☆☆☆

FULL

MED/FULL

MEDIUM

MILD

LIGHT

FLAVOR CHART 0=LEAST 5=MOST						
BITTER						
CHOCOLATE						
EARTHY						
FRUITY						
HERBAL						
LEATHER						
NUTTY						
SPICY						
SWEET						
TOFFEE						
TROPICAL						
VANILLA						
WOODY						

TASTE NOTES

Cigar
aficionado

CIGAR NAME:

MAKER: _____ **PRICE:** _____

ORIGIN: _____ **DATE:** _____

LENGTH: _____ **RING SIZE:** _____

SHAPE: _____ **BUY AGAIN?** _____

AFFIX CIGAR LABEL HERE

RATING
☆☆☆☆☆

FULL

MED/FULL

MEDIUM

MILD

LIGHT

FLAVOR CHART 0=LEAST 5=MOST					
BITTER					
CHOCOLATE					
EARTHY					
FRUITY					
HERBAL					
LEATHER					
NUTTY					
SPICY					
SWEET					
TOFFEE					
TROPICAL					
VANILLA					
WOODY					

TASTE NOTES

CIGAR NAME:

MAKER:		**PRICE:**	
ORIGIN:		**DATE:**	
LENGTH:		**RING SIZE:**	
SHAPE:		**BUY AGAIN?**	

AFFIX CIGAR LABEL HERE

RATING
☆☆☆☆☆

FULL

MED/FULL

MEDIUM

MILD

LIGHT

FLAVOR CHART 0=LEAST 5=MOST					
BITTER					
CHOCOLATE					
EARTHY					
FRUITY					
HERBAL					
LEATHER					
NUTTY					
SPICY					
SWEET					
TOFFEE					
TROPICAL					
VANILLA					
WOODY					

TASTE NOTES

A
Cigar
IN
HAND
IS BETTER THAN TWO
IN THE HUMIDOR

CIGAR NAME: _____

MAKER: _____ **PRICE:** _____

ORIGIN: _____ **DATE:** _____

LENGTH: _____ **RING SIZE:** _____

SHAPE: _____ **BUY AGAIN?** _____

```
         AFFIX CIGAR
         LABEL HERE
```

RATING
☆☆☆☆☆

FULL

MED/FULL

MEDIUM

MILD

LIGHT

FLAVOR CHART 0=LEAST 5=MOST						
BITTER						
CHOCOLATE						
EARTHY						
FRUITY						
HERBAL						
LEATHER						
NUTTY						
SPICY						
SWEET						
TOFFEE						
TROPICAL						
VANILLA						
WOODY						

TASTE NOTES

CIGAR NAME: _____

MAKER: _____ **PRICE:** _____

ORIGIN: _____ **DATE:** _____

LENGTH: _____ **RING SIZE:** _____

SHAPE: _____ **BUY AGAIN?** _____

AFFIX CIGAR LABEL HERE

RATING
☆☆☆☆☆

FULL

MED/FULL

MEDIUM

MILD

LIGHT

FLAVOR CHART 0=LEAST 5=MOST					
BITTER					
CHOCOLATE					
EARTHY					
FRUITY					
HERBAL					
LEATHER					
NUTTY					
SPICY					
SWEET					
TOFFEE					
TROPICAL					
VANILLA					
WOODY					

TASTE NOTES

me time

CIGAR NAME: _____

MAKER: _____ **PRICE:** _____

ORIGIN: _____ **DATE:** _____

LENGTH: _____ **RING SIZE:** _____

SHAPE: _____ **BUY AGAIN?** _____

AFFIX CIGAR LABEL HERE

RATING
☆☆☆☆☆

FULL

MED/FULL

MEDIUM

MILD

LIGHT

FLAVOR CHART 0=LEAST 5=MOST					
BITTER					
CHOCOLATE					
EARTHY					
FRUITY					
HERBAL					
LEATHER					
NUTTY					
SPICY					
SWEET					
TOFFEE					
TROPICAL					
VANILLA					
WOODY					

TASTE NOTES

REAL MEN SMOKE
CIGARS

CIGAR NAME: _____

MAKER: _____ **PRICE:** _____

ORIGIN: _____ **DATE:** _____

LENGTH: _____ **RING SIZE:** _____

SHAPE: _____ **BUY AGAIN?** _____

AFFIX CIGAR LABEL HERE

RATING
☆☆☆☆☆

FULL

MED/FULL

MEDIUM

MILD

LIGHT

FLAVOR CHART 0=LEAST 5=MOST						
BITTER						
CHOCOLATE						
EARTHY						
FRUITY						
HERBAL						
LEATHER						
NUTTY						
SPICY						
SWEET						
TOFFEE						
TROPICAL						
VANILLA						
WOODY						

TASTE NOTES

_____

_____

_____

_____

_____

_____

_____

_____

_____

_____

_____

_____

_____

_____

_____

_____

_____

_____

IF IT INVOLVES
Cigars
COUNT ME IN

CIGAR NAME: _____

MAKER: _____   **PRICE:** _____

ORIGIN: _____   **DATE:** _____

LENGTH: _____   **RING SIZE:** _____

SHAPE: _____   **BUY AGAIN?** _____

AFFIX CIGAR LABEL HERE

RATING
☆☆☆☆☆

FULL

MED/FULL

MEDIUM

MILD

LIGHT

FLAVOR CHART 0=LEAST 5=MOST						
BITTER						
CHOCOLATE						
EARTHY						
FRUITY						
HERBAL						
LEATHER						
NUTTY						
SPICY						
SWEET						
TOFFEE						
TROPICAL						
VANILLA						
WOODY						

TASTE NOTES

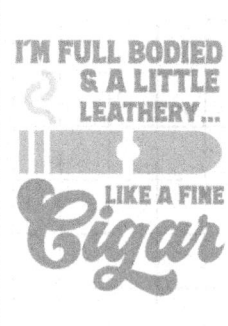

I'M FULL BODIED
& A LITTLE
LEATHERY...
LIKE A FINE
Cigar

CIGAR NAME: _____

MAKER: _____ **PRICE:** _____

ORIGIN: _____ **DATE:** _____

LENGTH: _____ **RING SIZE:** _____

SHAPE: _____ **BUY AGAIN?** _____

AFFIX CIGAR LABEL HERE

RATING
☆☆☆☆☆

FULL

MED/FULL

MEDIUM

MILD

LIGHT

FLAVOR CHART 0=LEAST 5=MOST					
BITTER					
CHOCOLATE					
EARTHY					
FRUITY					
HERBAL					
LEATHER					
NUTTY					
SPICY					
SWEET					
TOFFEE					
TROPICAL					
VANILLA					
WOODY					

TASTE NOTES

Cigar aficionado

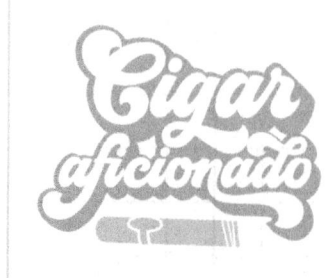

CIGAR NAME: _____

MAKER: _____ **PRICE:** _____

ORIGIN: _____ **DATE:** _____

LENGTH: _____ **RING SIZE:** _____

SHAPE: _____ **BUY AGAIN?** _____

AFFIX CIGAR LABEL HERE

RATING
☆☆☆☆☆

FULL

MED/FULL

MEDIUM

MILD

LIGHT

FLAVOR CHART 0=LEAST 5=MOST					
BITTER					
CHOCOLATE					
EARTHY					
FRUITY					
HERBAL					
LEATHER					
NUTTY					
SPICY					
SWEET					
TOFFEE					
TROPICAL					
VANILLA					
WOODY					

TASTE NOTES

_____

_____

_____

_____

_____

_____

_____

_____

_____

_____

_____

_____

_____

_____

_____

_____

They see me rollin'

CIGAR NAME: _____

MAKER: _____ **PRICE:** _____

ORIGIN: _____ **DATE:** _____

LENGTH: _____ **RING SIZE:** _____

SHAPE: _____ **BUY AGAIN?** _____

AFFIX CIGAR LABEL HERE

RATING
☆☆☆☆☆

FULL

MED/FULL

MEDIUM

MILD

LIGHT

FLAVOR CHART 0=LEAST 5=MOST						
BITTER						
CHOCOLATE						
EARTHY						
FRUITY						
HERBAL						
LEATHER						
NUTTY						
SPICY						
SWEET						
TOFFEE						
TROPICAL						
VANILLA						
WOODY						

TASTE NOTES

A Cigar IN HAND IS BETTER THAN TWO IN THE HUMIDOR

CIGAR NAME: _____

MAKER: _____ **PRICE:** _____

ORIGIN: _____ **DATE:** _____

LENGTH: _____ **RING SIZE:** _____

SHAPE: _____ **BUY AGAIN?** _____

AFFIX CIGAR LABEL HERE

RATING
☆☆☆☆☆

FULL

MED/FULL

MEDIUM

MILD

LIGHT

FLAVOR CHART 0=LEAST 5=MOST					
BITTER					
CHOCOLATE					
EARTHY					
FRUITY					
HERBAL					
LEATHER					
NUTTY					
SPICY					
SWEET					
TOFFEE					
TROPICAL					
VANILLA					
WOODY					

TASTE NOTES

CIGAR NAME: _____

MAKER: _____   **PRICE:** _____

ORIGIN: _____   **DATE:** _____

LENGTH: _____   **RING SIZE:** _____

SHAPE: _____   **BUY AGAIN?** _____

AFFIX CIGAR LABEL HERE

RATING
☆☆☆☆☆

FULL

MED/FULL

MEDIUM

MILD

LIGHT

FLAVOR CHART 0=LEAST 5=MOST						
BITTER						
CHOCOLATE						
EARTHY						
FRUITY						
HERBAL						
LEATHER						
NUTTY						
SPICY						
SWEET						
TOFFEE						
TROPICAL						
VANILLA						
WOODY						

TASTE NOTES

me time

CIGAR NAME:

MAKER:	**PRICE:**
ORIGIN:	**DATE:**
LENGTH:	**RING SIZE:**
SHAPE:	**BUY AGAIN?**

AFFIX CIGAR LABEL HERE

RATING
☆☆☆☆☆

FULL

MED/FULL

MEDIUM

MILD

LIGHT

FLAVOR CHART 0=LEAST 5=MOST						
BITTER						
CHOCOLATE						
EARTHY						
FRUITY						
HERBAL						
LEATHER						
NUTTY						
SPICY						
SWEET						
TOFFEE						
TROPICAL						
VANILLA						
WOODY						

TASTE NOTES

REAL MEN SMOKE

CIGARS

CIGAR NAME: _____

MAKER: _____ **PRICE:** _____

ORIGIN: _____ **DATE:** _____

LENGTH: _____ **RING SIZE:** _____

SHAPE: _____ **BUY AGAIN?** _____

AFFIX CIGAR LABEL HERE

RATING
☆☆☆☆☆

FULL

MED/FULL

MEDIUM

MILD

LIGHT

FLAVOR CHART 0=LEAST 5=MOST					
BITTER					
CHOCOLATE					
EARTHY					
FRUITY					
HERBAL					
LEATHER					
NUTTY					
SPICY					
SWEET					
TOFFEE					
TROPICAL					
VANILLA					
WOODY					

TASTE NOTES

IF IT INVOLVES Cigars COUNT ME IN

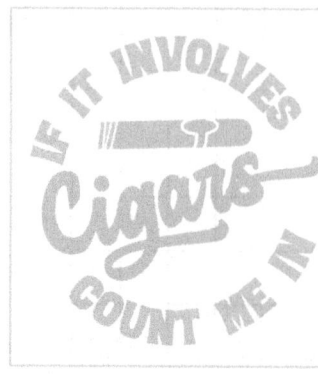

CIGAR NAME: _____

MAKER: _____ **PRICE:** _____

ORIGIN: _____ **DATE:** _____

LENGTH: _____ **RING SIZE:** _____

SHAPE: _____ **BUY AGAIN?** _____

AFFIX CIGAR LABEL HERE

RATING
☆☆☆☆☆

FULL

MED/FULL

MEDIUM

MILD

LIGHT

FLAVOR CHART 0=LEAST 5=MOST					
BITTER					
CHOCOLATE					
EARTHY					
FRUITY					
HERBAL					
LEATHER					
NUTTY					
SPICY					
SWEET					
TOFFEE					
TROPICAL					
VANILLA					
WOODY					

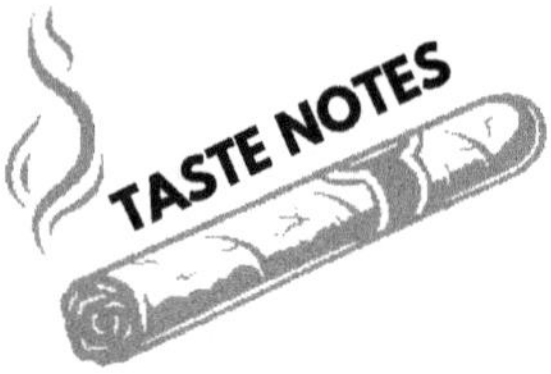
TASTE NOTES

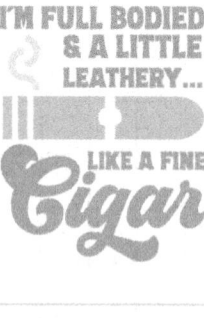

I'M FULL BODIED
& A LITTLE
LEATHERY...
LIKE A FINE
Cigar

CIGAR NAME: _____

MAKER: _____ **PRICE:** _____

ORIGIN: _____ **DATE:** _____

LENGTH: _____ **RING SIZE:** _____

SHAPE: _____ **BUY AGAIN?** _____

AFFIX CIGAR LABEL HERE

RATING
☆☆☆☆☆

FULL

MED/FULL

MEDIUM

MILD

LIGHT

FLAVOR CHART 0=LEAST 5=MOST						
BITTER						
CHOCOLATE						
EARTHY						
FRUITY						
HERBAL						
LEATHER						
NUTTY						
SPICY						
SWEET						
TOFFEE						
TROPICAL						
VANILLA						
WOODY						

TASTE NOTES

CIGAR NAME: _____

MAKER: _____ **PRICE:** _____

ORIGIN: _____ **DATE:** _____

LENGTH: _____ **RING SIZE:** _____

SHAPE: _____ **BUY AGAIN?** _____

AFFIX CIGAR LABEL HERE

RATING
☆☆☆☆☆

FULL

MED/FULL

MEDIUM

MILD

LIGHT

FLAVOR CHART 0=LEAST 5=MOST					
BITTER					
CHOCOLATE					
EARTHY					
FRUITY					
HERBAL					
LEATHER					
NUTTY					
SPICY					
SWEET					
TOFFEE					
TROPICAL					
VANILLA					
WOODY					

TASTE NOTES

_____

_____

_____

_____

_____

_____

_____

_____

_____

_____

_____

_____

_____

_____

_____

_____

_____

_____

They see me rollin'

CIGAR NAME: _____

MAKER: _____   **PRICE:** _____

ORIGIN: _____   **DATE:** _____

LENGTH: _____   **RING SIZE:** _____

SHAPE: _____   **BUY AGAIN?** _____

AFFIX CIGAR LABEL HERE

RATING
☆☆☆☆☆

FULL

MED/FULL

MEDIUM

MILD

LIGHT

FLAVOR CHART 0=LEAST 5=MOST						
BITTER						
CHOCOLATE						
EARTHY						
FRUITY						
HERBAL						
LEATHER						
NUTTY						
SPICY						
SWEET						
TOFFEE						
TROPICAL						
VANILLA						
WOODY						

TASTE NOTES

A **Cigar** IN HAND
IS BETTER THAN TWO
IN THE HUMIDOR

CIGAR NAME: _____

MAKER: _____   **PRICE:** _____

ORIGIN: _____   **DATE:** _____

LENGTH: _____   **RING SIZE:** _____

SHAPE: _____   **BUY AGAIN?** _____

AFFIX CIGAR LABEL HERE

RATING
☆☆☆☆☆

FULL

MED/FULL

MEDIUM

MILD

LIGHT

FLAVOR CHART 0=LEAST 5=MOST						
BITTER						
CHOCOLATE						
EARTHY						
FRUITY						
HERBAL						
LEATHER						
NUTTY						
SPICY						
SWEET						
TOFFEE						
TROPICAL						
VANILLA						
WOODY						

TASTE NOTES

CIGAR NAME: _____

MAKER: _____   **PRICE:** _____

ORIGIN: _____   **DATE:** _____

LENGTH: _____   **RING SIZE:** _____

SHAPE: _____   **BUY AGAIN?** _____

AFFIX CIGAR LABEL HERE

RATING
☆☆☆☆☆

FULL

MED/FULL

MEDIUM

MILD

LIGHT

FLAVOR CHART 0=LEAST 5=MOST					
BITTER					
CHOCOLATE					
EARTHY					
FRUITY					
HERBAL					
LEATHER					
NUTTY					
SPICY					
SWEET					
TOFFEE					
TROPICAL					
VANILLA					
WOODY					

TASTE NOTES

me time

CIGAR NAME: _____

MAKER: _____ **PRICE:** _____

ORIGIN: _____ **DATE:** _____

LENGTH: _____ **RING SIZE:** _____

SHAPE: _____ **BUY AGAIN?** _____

```
AFFIX CIGAR
LABEL HERE
```

RATING
☆☆☆☆☆

FULL

MED/FULL

MEDIUM

MILD

LIGHT

FLAVOR CHART 0=LEAST 5=MOST					
BITTER					
CHOCOLATE					
EARTHY					
FRUITY					
HERBAL					
LEATHER					
NUTTY					
SPICY					
SWEET					
TOFFEE					
TROPICAL					
VANILLA					
WOODY					

TASTE NOTES

REAL MEN SMOKE
CIGARS

CIGAR NAME: _____

MAKER: _____ **PRICE:** _____

ORIGIN: _____ **DATE:** _____

LENGTH: _____ **RING SIZE:** _____

SHAPE: _____ **BUY AGAIN?** _____

AFFIX CIGAR LABEL HERE

RATING
☆☆☆☆☆

| FULL |
| MED/FULL |
| MEDIUM |
| MILD |
| LIGHT |

FLAVOR CHART 0=LEAST 5=MOST						
BITTER						
CHOCOLATE						
EARTHY						
FRUITY						
HERBAL						
LEATHER						
NUTTY						
SPICY						
SWEET						
TOFFEE						
TROPICAL						
VANILLA						
WOODY						

TASTE NOTES

IF IT INVOLVES Cigars COUNT ME IN

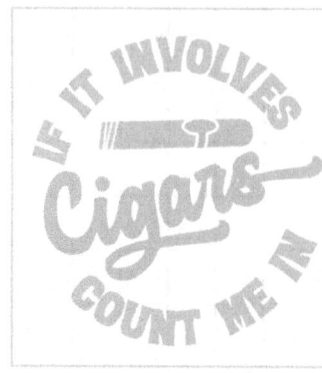

CIGAR NAME: _____

MAKER: _____	**PRICE:** _____
ORIGIN: _____	**DATE:** _____
LENGTH: _____	**RING SIZE:** _____
SHAPE: _____	**BUY AGAIN?** _____

AFFIX CIGAR LABEL HERE

RATING	FLAVOR CHART 0=LEAST 5=MOST					
☆☆☆☆☆	**BITTER**					
	CHOCOLATE					
	EARTHY					
	FRUITY					
FULL	**HERBAL**					
MED/FULL	**LEATHER**					
MEDIUM	**NUTTY**					
	SPICY					
MILD	**SWEET**					
	TOFFEE					
LIGHT	**TROPICAL**					
	VANILLA					
	WOODY					

TASTE NOTES

I'M FULL BODIED
& A LITTLE
LEATHERY...

LIKE A FINE
Cigar

CIGAR NAME: _____

MAKER: _____   **PRICE:** _____

ORIGIN: _____   **DATE:** _____

LENGTH: _____   **RING SIZE:** _____

SHAPE: _____   **BUY AGAIN?** _____

```
AFFIX CIGAR
LABEL HERE
```

RATING
☆☆☆☆☆

FULL

MED/FULL

MEDIUM

MILD

LIGHT

FLAVOR CHART 0=LEAST 5=MOST					
BITTER					
CHOCOLATE					
EARTHY					
FRUITY					
HERBAL					
LEATHER					
NUTTY					
SPICY					
SWEET					
TOFFEE					
TROPICAL					
VANILLA					
WOODY					

TASTE NOTES

CIGAR NAME: _____

MAKER: _____   **PRICE:** _____

ORIGIN: _____   **DATE:** _____

LENGTH: _____   **RING SIZE:** _____

SHAPE: _____   **BUY AGAIN?** _____

AFFIX CIGAR LABEL HERE

RATING
☆☆☆☆☆

FULL

MED/FULL

MEDIUM

MILD

LIGHT

FLAVOR CHART 0=LEAST 5=MOST					
BITTER					
CHOCOLATE					
EARTHY					
FRUITY					
HERBAL					
LEATHER					
NUTTY					
SPICY					
SWEET					
TOFFEE					
TROPICAL					
VANILLA					
WOODY					

TASTE NOTES

CIGAR NAME:

MAKER: _____ **PRICE:** _____

ORIGIN: _____ **DATE:** _____

LENGTH: _____ **RING SIZE:** _____

SHAPE: _____ **BUY AGAIN?** _____

AFFIX CIGAR LABEL HERE

RATING
☆☆☆☆☆

FULL

MED/FULL

MEDIUM

MILD

LIGHT

FLAVOR CHART 0=LEAST 5=MOST						
BITTER						
CHOCOLATE						
EARTHY						
FRUITY						
HERBAL						
LEATHER						
NUTTY						
SPICY						
SWEET						
TOFFEE						
TROPICAL						
VANILLA						
WOODY						

TASTE NOTES

_____
_____
_____
_____
_____
_____
_____
_____
_____
_____
_____
_____
_____
_____
_____
_____
_____
_____
_____
_____

A Cigar IN HAND IS BETTER THAN TWO IN THE HUMIDOR

CIGAR NAME: _____

MAKER: _____   **PRICE:** _____

ORIGIN: _____   **DATE:** _____

LENGTH: _____   **RING SIZE:** _____

SHAPE: _____   **BUY AGAIN?** _____

AFFIX CIGAR LABEL HERE

RATING
☆☆☆☆☆

FULL

MED/FULL

MEDIUM

MILD

LIGHT

FLAVOR CHART 0=LEAST 5=MOST					
BITTER					
CHOCOLATE					
EARTHY					
FRUITY					
HERBAL					
LEATHER					
NUTTY					
SPICY					
SWEET					
TOFFEE					
TROPICAL					
VANILLA					
WOODY					

TASTE NOTES

CIGAR NAME: _____

MAKER: _____ **PRICE:** _____

ORIGIN: _____ **DATE:** _____

LENGTH: _____ **RING SIZE:** _____

SHAPE: _____ **BUY AGAIN?** _____

AFFIX CIGAR LABEL HERE

RATING
☆☆☆☆☆

FULL

MED/FULL

MEDIUM

MILD

LIGHT

FLAVOR CHART 0=LEAST 5=MOST					
BITTER					
CHOCOLATE					
EARTHY					
FRUITY					
HERBAL					
LEATHER					
NUTTY					
SPICY					
SWEET					
TOFFEE					
TROPICAL					
VANILLA					
WOODY					

TASTE NOTES

me time

CIGAR NAME: _____

MAKER: _____ **PRICE:** _____

ORIGIN: _____ **DATE:** _____

LENGTH: _____ **RING SIZE:** _____

SHAPE: _____ **BUY AGAIN?** _____

AFFIX CIGAR LABEL HERE

RATING
☆☆☆☆☆

FULL

MED/FULL

MEDIUM

MILD

LIGHT

FLAVOR CHART 0=LEAST 5=MOST						
BITTER						
CHOCOLATE						
EARTHY						
FRUITY						
HERBAL						
LEATHER						
NUTTY						
SPICY						
SWEET						
TOFFEE						
TROPICAL						
VANILLA						
WOODY						

TASTE NOTES

REAL MEN SMOKE
CIGARS

CIGAR NAME: _____

MAKER: _____   **PRICE:** _____

ORIGIN: _____   **DATE:** _____

LENGTH: _____   **RING SIZE:** _____

SHAPE: _____   **BUY AGAIN?** _____

AFFIX CIGAR LABEL HERE

RATING

☆☆☆☆☆

FULL

MED/FULL

MEDIUM

MILD

LIGHT

FLAVOR CHART 0=LEAST 5=MOST					
BITTER					
CHOCOLATE					
EARTHY					
FRUITY					
HERBAL					
LEATHER					
NUTTY					
SPICY					
SWEET					
TOFFEE					
TROPICAL					
VANILLA					
WOODY					

TASTE NOTES

IF IT INVOLVES

Cigars

COUNT ME IN

CIGAR NAME: _____

MAKER: _____ **PRICE:** _____

ORIGIN: _____ **DATE:** _____

LENGTH: _____ **RING SIZE:** _____

SHAPE: _____ **BUY AGAIN?** _____

AFFIX CIGAR LABEL HERE

RATING
☆☆☆☆☆

FULL

MED/FULL

MEDIUM

MILD

LIGHT

FLAVOR CHART 0=LEAST 5=MOST						
BITTER						
CHOCOLATE						
EARTHY						
FRUITY						
HERBAL						
LEATHER						
NUTTY						
SPICY						
SWEET						
TOFFEE						
TROPICAL						
VANILLA						
WOODY						

TASTE NOTES

I'M FULL BODIED & A LITTLE LEATHERY... LIKE A FINE *Cigar*

CIGAR NAME: _____

MAKER: _____ **PRICE:** _____

ORIGIN: _____ **DATE:** _____

LENGTH: _____ **RING SIZE:** _____

SHAPE: _____ **BUY AGAIN?** _____

```
┌──────────────────────────────┐
│       AFFIX CIGAR            │
│       LABEL HERE            │
└──────────────────────────────┘
```

RATING
☆☆☆☆☆

FULL

MED/FULL

MEDIUM

MILD

LIGHT

FLAVOR CHART 0=LEAST 5=MOST						
BITTER						
CHOCOLATE						
EARTHY						
FRUITY						
HERBAL						
LEATHER						
NUTTY						
SPICY						
SWEET						
TOFFEE						
TROPICAL						
VANILLA						
WOODY						

TASTE NOTES

_____

_____

_____

_____

_____

_____

_____

_____

_____

_____

_____

_____

_____

_____

_____

_____

_____

CIGAR NAME: _____

MAKER: _____ **PRICE:** _____

ORIGIN: _____ **DATE:** _____

LENGTH: _____ **RING SIZE:** _____

SHAPE: _____ **BUY AGAIN?** _____

AFFIX CIGAR LABEL HERE

RATING
☆☆☆☆☆

FULL

MED/FULL

MEDIUM

MILD

LIGHT

FLAVOR CHART 0=LEAST 5=MOST					
BITTER					
CHOCOLATE					
EARTHY					
FRUITY					
HERBAL					
LEATHER					
NUTTY					
SPICY					
SWEET					
TOFFEE					
TROPICAL					
VANILLA					
WOODY					

TASTE NOTES

They see me rollin'

CIGAR NAME: _____

MAKER: _____ **PRICE:** _____

ORIGIN: _____ **DATE:** _____

LENGTH: _____ **RING SIZE:** _____

SHAPE: _____ **BUY AGAIN?** _____

AFFIX CIGAR LABEL HERE

RATING
☆☆☆☆☆

FULL

MED/FULL

MEDIUM

MILD

LIGHT

FLAVOR CHART 0=LEAST 5=MOST					
BITTER					
CHOCOLATE					
EARTHY					
FRUITY					
HERBAL					
LEATHER					
NUTTY					
SPICY					
SWEET					
TOFFEE					
TROPICAL					
VANILLA					
WOODY					

TASTE NOTES

_____

_____

_____

_____

_____

_____

_____

_____

_____

_____

_____

_____

_____

_____

_____

_____

_____

A
Cigar
IN
HAND
IS BETTER THAN TWO
IN THE HUMIDOR

CIGAR NAME: _____

MAKER: _____ **PRICE:** _____

ORIGIN: _____ **DATE:** _____

LENGTH: _____ **RING SIZE:** _____

SHAPE: _____ **BUY AGAIN?** _____

AFFIX CIGAR LABEL HERE

RATING
☆ ☆ ☆ ☆ ☆

FULL

MED/FULL

MEDIUM

MILD

LIGHT

FLAVOR CHART 0=LEAST 5=MOST						
BITTER						
CHOCOLATE						
EARTHY						
FRUITY						
HERBAL						
LEATHER						
NUTTY						
SPICY						
SWEET						
TOFFEE						
TROPICAL						
VANILLA						
WOODY						

TASTE NOTES

CIGAR NAME: _____

MAKER: _____ **PRICE:** _____

ORIGIN: _____ **DATE:** _____

LENGTH: _____ **RING SIZE:** _____

SHAPE: _____ **BUY AGAIN?** _____

AFFIX CIGAR LABEL HERE

RATING
☆☆☆☆☆

FULL

MED/FULL

MEDIUM

MILD

LIGHT

FLAVOR CHART 0=LEAST 5=MOST					
BITTER					
CHOCOLATE					
EARTHY					
FRUITY					
HERBAL					
LEATHER					
NUTTY					
SPICY					
SWEET					
TOFFEE					
TROPICAL					
VANILLA					
WOODY					

TASTE NOTES

me time

CIGAR NAME: _____

MAKER: _____   **PRICE:** _____

ORIGIN: _____   **DATE:** _____

LENGTH: _____   **RING SIZE:** _____

SHAPE: _____   **BUY AGAIN?** _____

AFFIX CIGAR LABEL HERE

RATING
☆☆☆☆☆

FULL

MED/FULL

MEDIUM

MILD

LIGHT

FLAVOR CHART 0=LEAST 5=MOST					
BITTER					
CHOCOLATE					
EARTHY					
FRUITY					
HERBAL					
LEATHER					
NUTTY					
SPICY					
SWEET					
TOFFEE					
TROPICAL					
VANILLA					
WOODY					

TASTE NOTES

REAL MEN SMOKE
CIGARS

CIGAR NAME: _____

MAKER: _____ **PRICE:** _____

ORIGIN: _____ **DATE:** _____

LENGTH: _____ **RING SIZE:** _____

SHAPE: _____ **BUY AGAIN?** _____

AFFIX CIGAR LABEL HERE

RATING

☆☆☆☆☆

FULL

MED/FULL

MEDIUM

MILD

LIGHT

FLAVOR CHART 0=LEAST 5=MOST						
BITTER						
CHOCOLATE						
EARTHY						
FRUITY						
HERBAL						
LEATHER						
NUTTY						
SPICY						
SWEET						
TOFFEE						
TROPICAL						
VANILLA						
WOODY						

TASTE NOTES

CIGAR NAME: _____

MAKER: _____ **PRICE:** _____

ORIGIN: _____ **DATE:** _____

LENGTH: _____ **RING SIZE:** _____

SHAPE: _____ **BUY AGAIN?** _____

AFFIX CIGAR LABEL HERE

RATING
☆☆☆☆☆

FULL

MED/FULL

MEDIUM

MILD

LIGHT

FLAVOR CHART 0=LEAST 5=MOST					
BITTER					
CHOCOLATE					
EARTHY					
FRUITY					
HERBAL					
LEATHER					
NUTTY					
SPICY					
SWEET					
TOFFEE					
TROPICAL					
VANILLA					
WOODY					

TASTE NOTES

I'M FULL BODIED & A LITTLE LEATHERY...

LIKE A FINE Cigar

CIGAR NAME: _____

MAKER: _____ **PRICE:** _____

ORIGIN: _____ **DATE:** _____

LENGTH: _____ **RING SIZE:** _____

SHAPE: _____ **BUY AGAIN?** _____

AFFIX CIGAR LABEL HERE

RATING
☆☆☆☆☆

FULL

MED/FULL

MEDIUM

MILD

LIGHT

FLAVOR CHART 0=LEAST 5=MOST					
BITTER					
CHOCOLATE					
EARTHY					
FRUITY					
HERBAL					
LEATHER					
NUTTY					
SPICY					
SWEET					
TOFFEE					
TROPICAL					
VANILLA					
WOODY					

TASTE NOTES

_____

CIGAR NAME: _____

MAKER: _____ **PRICE:** _____

ORIGIN: _____ **DATE:** _____

LENGTH: _____ **RING SIZE:** _____

SHAPE: _____ **BUY AGAIN?** _____

AFFIX CIGAR LABEL HERE

RATING	FLAVOR CHART 0=LEAST 5=MOST					
☆☆☆☆☆	BITTER					
	CHOCOLATE					
	EARTHY					
	FRUITY					
FULL	HERBAL					
MED/FULL	LEATHER					
	NUTTY					
MEDIUM	SPICY					
	SWEET					
MILD	TOFFEE					
	TROPICAL					
LIGHT	VANILLA					
	WOODY					

"There's something about smoking a cigar that feels like a celebration. It's like a fine wine. There's a quality, a workmanship, a passion that goes into the smoking of a fine cigar."

Demi Moore

Made in the USA
Las Vegas, NV
06 December 2020

12206291R00069